# WEEKEND RETREATS

# WEEKEND RETREATS

By Susanna Salk

———

*Rizzoli*
NEW YORK

# CONTENTS

# INTRODUCTION

I am lucky enough to live year-round in a rural place where many flock to weekend. I never have had to pack a car for the long ride out on Friday night nor feel the ominous gloom that Sunday afternoon casts no matter how sunny the skies.

I'll also never know the bliss that the Friday-afternoon escape surely affords those who make the faithful journey week after week: watching the blinking lights of Manhattan recede as you slowly become enveloped by the soft darkness that only nights in the country bring. Of appreciating your driveway and the familiar sounds it makes as your wheels hurry up its path; of turning on the lights and shaking out the calm that has settled inside since you last left but also allowing that calm to settle into you.

With so many great places to hurry toward to find that dependable calm and pleasure of a second home, how did I pick these twenty-five weekend retreats to celebrate? I gravitated to each the way you would an intriguing stranger at a crowded party who warmly smiles and makes room for you on the sofa so you can swap life

opposite: A row of chairs await a lazy afternoon lounging by a pond in Connecticut.

stories. There is no small talk with any of these houses; they are all soul and depth. And while their walls and roofs shelter their owners from the elements, the ultimate relationship among setting, building, and human is seamless.

In most instances the people who bought these retreats were rescuers, saving the place from years of neglect so it could act as a weekly resuscitator and return the favor. In every instance the restoring, refurbishing, and decorating were acts of intense love, often performed on a small budget and with a large leap of faith. No objects or furniture were ever purchased for mere décor or functionality. From plank to picture frame, each element has a story to tell that gives it a compelling a raison d'être.

All these houses have a reverential respect for nature and acknowledge that the hills, lakes, farms, and fields around them came first. None of the houses nor the people who live in them care about pretense or taking exclusionary measures like tall hedges and walls. This is about bringing life in. And they do so with family, children, friends, animals, or sometimes just precious solitude. Simply put, after meeting them just once, I wanted to retreat to all these places alongside their owners. I wanted to help gather firewood, bake

opposite: The Winberg/ Shewer entry hall is the ideal setting for whimsical entrances and exits.

above: At the McEvoy house there is a bed for every guest, no matter how small.

bread, light candles, sing songs around a campfire, scour local flea markets, and mulch gardens. These houses hold deliciously rich and simple memories that wind and bind the inhabitants like life rings on a tree.

Great design does this to you: its joyful spirit is infectious. It always makes you want to explore, ponder, and put your feet up on the coffee table and see how life takes place there. These are places where hosts encourage you to have a second glass of red wine, their glorious white rug be damned and praised. After all, it is the weekend, and weekends are when we should take out our hopes and dreams and allow them to dance around.

The people in these homes don't just understand that, they celebrate it. At all these front doors, when you cross the threshold, you are embraced.

# PATCHWORK GLORY

New Kingston, NEW YORK

PHOTOGRAPHS BY MAURA MCEVOY

I t had asbestos siding, dark hallways, and no fireplace, but for photographer Maura McEvoy it was love at first sight as soon as she set eyes on her 1864 "eyebrow Colonial" nestled in the Catskills area of New York State.

The house, after all, sat on 150 glorious acres complete with a quarter-acre swimming pond and a "perfectly plumb" three-story barn. And so began a three-year renovation journey that Maura, her husband, Steven, their young daughter, Oona, and dachshund, Meme, embarked upon with a feverish determination to bring beauty, comfort, and property views to their weekend retreat. Maura would spend hours drafting ways to reconfigure the rooms to let in more light, which ultimately resulted in putting shed roofs on all the bedrooms upstairs. This then inspired a domino-style makeover of the downstairs: walls

opposite: In the dining room, a dark oak table and chairs formerly from a library now seat friends and family.

opposite: The fireplace mantel is an old barn beam donated from a neighbor. Bamboo chairs were found at a flea market in Maine and then covered in leather by a good friend. The curtains are from McEvoy's grandmother's house in Maine.

this page: McEvoy's daughter Oona lounges on her favorite daybed with a good book. McEvoy designed the patchwork linen curtains herself.

were eliminated, bathrooms moved, the kitchen ripped out. Inspiration often came from the surrounding area: Steven found a piece of cherry wood at a nearby salvage trove, and it became the ideal island countertop. A fireplace was created and outfitted with a mantel beam made from wood salvaged from a neighbor's collapsed barn. Local flea markets, auctions, and antiques stores were scoured with an expert eye. Maura's experience as a stylist taught her to always buy in bulk, and before long, the house was decorated in a style she describes as "whimsy, chaos, and thrift. Always there is a jolt of color, as I feel it's the driving force in a room."

Besides color, both Maura and Steven are driven by certain textures. "Steven loves wood, and my thing is fabric." In fact, much of the windows are covered with the remnants she is constantly scouting for and then bringing to life in unique ways: for the multicolored linen cur-

15

opposite: The upstairs was renovated using beams from a neighbor's dismantled barn on the walls and ceilings. McEvoy took the photo of Oona and blew it up onto canvas.

tains in the living room, she arranged paint sample cards in a pattern and then had a seamstress sew the corresponding fabric into being.

Naturally, then, the first thing Maura does when she enters the house is open all the curtains, signaling the start of busy weekends filled with friends and family who gather in anticipation of Steven's home-cooked Italian dinners. If it is warm enough, they will dine in the outdoor room built of fieldstones and barn beams, which offers sweeping views of the Catskills and where hanging Chinese lanterns glow red at night. For entertainment, there are games of charades, or watching nephew Albert performing flips off the floating dock into the pond. If the weather is colder, a bonfire is lit in a nearby pit and everyone gathers around for wine and song.

And at the end of the weekend, Maura often finds herself winding

16

opposite: The cupboard
is original to the house
and filled with dishes
and favorite assorted
objects like a penguin
martini shaker.

this page: A birdhouse
sits atop a barn beam
while a leprechaun the
family spray-painted
silver watches the day
pass by.

her way from the pond to the house marveling at a view she can call
her own. "We let the fields go wild and just mow paths through them."
Her landscaping philosophy—and her overall design sense—seeks to
create a harmonious balance between the natural and the man-made.
The result is a home that is a cozy amalgamation of happenstance and
passionate intent. "You can't agonize over making mistakes: you must
appreciate that you are creating something that is handmade—that is
where the beauty shines."

**19**

# SET FOR DREAMS

Morris, CONNECTICUT

PHOTOGRAPHS BY OBERTO GILI

opposite: The wisteria-covered screened porch off the dining room overlooks the pool and poolhouse in the distance. Chinese lanterns and a Morris chair from the film *Sea of Love,* are paired with vintage rattan chairs and a small side table from the film *Unfaithful.*

A s master scenic artists for feature films ranging from Steven Spielberg's *War of the Worlds* to Martin Scorsese's *The Departed*, Bob Topol and Tony Trotta continually transform what is imagined into celluloid reality through painting, sculpting, and mold making to give it history and character. But for their own weekend house, they looked to the fantasy sets they created to turn a tiny, neglected 1940s log-sided lake house complete with lime-green shag carpet into a retreat reminiscent of their favorite 1945 film, *The Enchanted Cottage.* "We wanted to re-create that same feeling of a refuge for ourselves," says Topol, who met Trotta on a film set in Atlanta twenty years ago, "like we were in our own movie." Bringing the same thoughtful, passionate collaboration to the site in Connecticut as they do to sets around the world, Topol and Trotta transformed Redbrush

opposite: In the winter dining room, Adirondack rustic meets Oriental fantasy. Chairs are from *Cider House Rules*, and the ivory tusk is from Africa from Trotta's days as a Peace Corps volunteer. The chandelier was handmade by Topol and Trotta.

this page: On the dining room sideboard, eucalyptus-covered obelisks are from the film *Hannibal*. The clock was found in Brooklyn while shooting *The Departed*. The ceramic compote came from an antique store in Hudson, New York, while shooting *Nobody's Fool*.

Hill (aptly named for the brush that grows all around the property) into a property worthy of movie-star close-ups, with a quiet drama that is Adirondack Style meets Brideshead Revisited.

It was privacy of the land that entranced them first. At the end of a meandering driveway, surrounded by meadows, streams, and a land trust, Redbrush Hill was the ideal contrast to their modernist Chelsea apartment. "We wanted the antithesis to New York," says Topol, who studied under famed scenic designer Lester Polakov, "a real period New England house." They immediately added a lodge-inspired din-

ing room wall-papered with Clarence House's "Papier Japonese" and a fairy-tale screened porch insulated with Japanese honeysuckle. Despite their elegant embellishments, however, the house was still too small for adequate entertaining.

Luckily there came a Cecil B. DeMille–worthy vision: to turn their original cottage into the guest wing and library so that it looked like a later addition behind the new two-story shingle-style addition they were about to create.

They immediately established a list of mandates: no part of the

opposite: The patio off the kitchen looks over to the potting shed. The table is from the orphanage dining room in *Cider House Rules* and the chairs once filled the stadium on *A League of Their Own*.

above: Inspired by the slats of wood and exposed beams from a cottage they rented in the Caribbean, Topol and Trotta created a pool house that is both quirky and chic. Trotta's mother embroidered the pillows and Topol painted the nautical sign above the window.

house could look new; doors in every room must open to the outdoors; there would be fireplaces in all common rooms and in the master bedroom; the dining room and kitchen would be of post-and-beam construction; the house would feature groove doors and hammered wrought-iron hardware throughout.

After creating a Georgian-style living room with symmetrical French doors and transom windows, it was time to fill in with mood: Topol painted a romantic screen based on a Georgian period room from the Metropolitan Museum of Art for the corner, and, nearby, Trotta added a Congo mask from his days in the Peace Corps. They then gave the dining room a rustic feel by making one wall all log and staining it with Minwax Early American Finish. For rosy-hued windows like the ones in the Brooklyn church where they had shot Spike Lee's *Clockers*, they fashioned their own stained-glass technique using French lacquers. A bounty of other props acquired from twenty years on movie sets found a permanent place off camera, and look as though they have always been personal possessions. Sometimes Mother Nature pitched in to the creative process: when two beautiful birch trees fell during a storm, Topol and Trotta simply brought them inside to fashion them into a delicate arch that still adorns the hallway and echoes the surrounding serenity.

Outside, they created a summer entertaining area with a reflecting pool and a wisteria-covered pool house inspired by the Rodin Museum in Philadelphia, where they lived while shooting Jonathan Demme's *Beloved*. Standing guard nearby are giant Balinese flags atop bamboo branches. "We were definitely thinking cinematically when we put them in," recalls Topol. Now guests linger like extras on the set of a film that no one, including its auteurs, wants to end. "We travel so much, we like to get back home and catch up to our dreams."

# NATURAL WONDER

Garrison, NEW YORK

PHOTOGRAPHS BY WILLIAM ABRANOWICZ

"Here we can give our kids the opportunity to witness the wonder of everything from insects to stars," says architect Adam Yarinsky of why he and his wife, Amy Weisser, chose this Hudson Highlands locale to provide Will (age ten) and Anna (seven) the ultimate nature observatory. Situated in Garrison, New York, accessed by a historic unpaved road and bound by public parkland on two sides, the buildings and grounds are on three levels that step down the hillside and integrate with the surrounding forest. Built as two identically dimensioned rectangular boxes, the house consists of an upper level that contains the living areas and an entry garden and a lower level that contains the family quarters and outdoor sitting areas. Everywhere, the relationship between the natural and the man-made is harmonious: views thread through the house, in and then out again,

opposite: The house, composed of two rectangular blocks terraced into a hillside, overlooks a meadow and is surrounded by a forest.

this page: Open to the view of the trees beyond, the living area centers on a Danish wood-burning stove and a walnut plank coffee table designed and built by the cabinetmaker Reed Karen.

opposite: A favorite print of a leaf by Ellsworth Kelly is homage to the natural setting, while the furnishings are a combination of contemporary and vintage midcentury modern pieces.

opposite: Detail of walnut plank dining table, with white-washed maple cabinetry and stainless steel appliances in kitchen beyond.

and its narrow width and orientation allows southern sunlight to pour into every nook and cranny. Throughout, says Yarinsky, who designed and decorated the house with Weisser, "matter-of-fact materials are used with precision of dimension and detail." Smooth concrete floors "emphasize the flow of space," and are warm underfoot thanks to radiant hot water tubing. Suspended Sheetrock ceilings in the main areas appear to float away from the interior walls, while exterior walls clad in corrugated aluminum reflect nature's ever-changing show outside.

The furnishings provide further frames for the view and the people who come to admire it. Alvar Aalto birch stools, Mies van der Rohe leather chairs, and earth-toned upholstery are warm and inviting and scaled to suit the loftlike openness of the space. Cabinetmaker Reed Karen was commissioned to build a dining room table of oiled walnut with a stainless-steel base. "Saturday-night dinner around the table— with guests or just the four of us," says Weisser, "allows us all to catch our breath and focus on each other. This fuels us for the week ahead."

The family enjoys each season here and revels in how the rocky

33

opposite: The dining terrace is partially enclosed by the corrugated metal wall of the living room wing and the red painted cement wall of the bedroom wing.

this page: Anna and Will in the loftlike living space.

hillside and the meadows, the streams and the ridge, take turns revealing themselves.

Weekend activities include exploring the nearby parks on foot or cross-country skis or staying indoors for extensive cooking sessions in the open kitchen area, with the kids as chefs and local produce as ingredients. Yarinsky explains, "A house should participate in the life of its inhabitants in ways that enrich their daily experience."

# CAMP COMPOUND

Kent, CONNECTICUT

PHOTOGRAPHS BY MATTHEW HRANEK

Formerly a children's summer camp, the lakeside family compound of interior designer Alexandra Champalimaud and her husband, Bruce Schnitzer, still functions as a kind of massive play area where they and generations of their extended family come every weekend to celebrate the joys of living alongside a hundred-acre lake in northwestern Connecticut. Bruce and Alexandra discovered the property twenty-three years ago, and the original three hundred acres was then subdivided with the intention of creating a lake association that would vigorously preserve the natural landscape and health of the lake. So while laughter and splashing is a constant noise, the one thing you won't hear is the sound of motor boats or jet skis. Nor television. "Thanks to my parents, it's still very much a pre-Pilgrim feel here," says their son, Anthony, who retreats faithfully every weekend.

When they found it, the property was dotted with approximately fifty-five buildings, and the seven that were kept had to be drastically restored and reworked for the family, not to mention winterized. But that didn't mean erasing the spirited history of its original occupants. The current kitchen, which used to function as a dressing room for the camp's theater productions, still bears the graffiti accumulated during its backstage life, and campers' stickers still decorate many of the rafters

opposite: National flags represent the various citizenships held by family members.

this page: The exterior of the theater with re-created camp lettering.

opposite: Accumulated possessions are camp appropriate, including a Panama hat, often worn on stage.

The Champalimaud
family decorated the
former camp them-
selves with the inten-
tion of "expressing
the nature of the place
yet not wanting it to
be too rustic or dark."

this page: Sometimes
nature provides the
most elegant hardware.

opposite: Summer life
here is about enjoying
cool breezes
and nature's harvest.

above. The 7,000-square-foot theater room is "the purest expression of the camp then and now," says Alexandra. Its stage regularly hosts live family and friends' bands and even was the setting for the wedding of the eldest brother, Lopo, and his wife, Sandrine. The master bedroom is in the theater annex, and has the luxury of being only footsteps from the water's edge. A series of guest room annexes and living areas all bear names that reflect their prior status: "Feeling Better" (formerly the infirmary), "the Boathouse," and "the Music Room."

The family decorated the interior themselves, intending "to express the nature of the place," says Anthony. "It's authentic but not overly rustic or dark." Branches hold the shower curtain, and vintage fans and pheasant feathers serve as decorative touches, giving the rooms a serene timelessness. Says Alexandra of her design philosophy here: "The style, if you can call it that, is simplified Adirondack, bark and all." Even the pine walls play a part as they reflect the warm, amber light at day's end.

During the summer, the pristine waters of the lake offer restorative qualities, as do the abundant gatherings over long outdoor lunches and wine.

"Fall is the work season," says Anthony. "We tend to the woods, make bonfires, and chainsaw. Guests enjoy chainsawing as much as tennis and sailing in the warmer months." Winter allows cross-country skiing around the lake and skating across it. No matter what the time, guests flock to a place that offers protection from weekday stress and obligations. "Everyone is on their own to do as they please," says Bruce. "It's a place for relaxation and peace."

# PREFAB RETREAT

Catskills Mountains, NEW YORK

PHOTOGRAPHS BY MATTHEW HRANEK

When Matthew and Yolanda Hranek set out to create their dream weekend retreat, they didn't initially expect that it would arrive in four large containers at Newark International Airport. In fact, when they first bought their pastoral 130-acre property near Hankins, New York, two years earlier, they interviewed dozens of architects in hopes to build it from scratch but always ended up frustrated that the proposed sketches weren't matching existing budgets.

"I had been obsessed with prefab architecture since college," admits Matthew, a photographer, "but I never dreamed I'd be able to ever experience it firsthand." Then, on assignment in Milan, he met Oscar Kauffmann, a prefab impresario who had just built a four-story prefab townhouse there, which Hranek had been sent to shoot. The men shared such similar design obsessions and aesthetics that, when

opposite: The prefab house glows like a welcoming fire in the winter night.

opposite: In the living area, cookbooks and art books share shelves. The family wanted the house to be an homage to the middle European country houses they love.

Hranek later sent Kauffmann a picture of his New York land site, Kauffman promptly returned the image with a proposed prefab house dropped in as seamlessly as if it had always existed there. "Stylistically, it was exactly how I had envisioned it," recalls Hranek, still clearly dazzled by their stylistic ESP. "It was Alpine style meets Mies van der Rohe with just the right dash of Marcel Breuer."

Matthew and Yolanda (then six months pregnant) promptly jumped on a plane to Austria and solidified the deal by designing the house à la carte: from its forty-foot window frontage to the oak veneer interior walls and ceiling.

The house arrived seven months later as planks of pressure-treated dense wood material that were insulated and spray-painted. Five Austrians then erected it, like a giant Lego set, over the course of four days. Hranek oversaw the production, marveling at their efficiency when he wasn't chuckling at the thought of realizing his dream so precisely.

Once built, the family outfitted the rooms with the eclectic and worldly furniture they had amassed over the years. "I had always had this classic midcentury modern vernacular in mind," says Matthew of his décor aspirations. Thrift-store chairs are roommates with a Jens Risom credenza Matthew rescued from IBM and a vintage Dunbar table Yolanda found in Manhattan. An enormous sheepskin rug is a personal favorite of Walter, their Jack Russell terrier. And four-year-old Clara loves to use the expansive eating and living space as her ballet studio. When her parents aren't watching her practice pirouettes,

48

opposite: A Hans
Wegner day bed with
custom felt bed is the
perfect perch to watch
a snowy day unfold.

this page: A Jens Risom
credenza helps display
flea market finds
like vintage crystal
decanters. The vintage
antlers take their
cues inspired from an
eighteenth-century
Scottish hunting house.

opposite: The living
room view with
its custom felt rug
and Dunbar coffee
table sets a tone
that is both modern
and welcoming.

this page: A still life
with an Arabia pitcher,
Danish bowl, and
turkey feathers from
the property.

this page: In the guest room, a Nessen lamp brightens bed linens and a vintage Hermes wood box.

opposite: In the dining area, utilitarian comfort meets style with a table designed by Hienz Ruescher Tischlerei surrounded by vintage Thonet schoolhouse chairs.

they are engaging in their other favorite weekend activity: doing noth-ing. "We never make a commitment to any activity. This is our retreat from urban life, and we come to restore ourselves," explains Yolanda. Yet their weekends are full of seasonal cooking, drinking, swimming, and all the pleasures that being so linked to nature brings. "The one thing we refuse to allow here is a television," says Matthew. "There's just too much to see outside."

# WHIMSY AND COMFORT

New Preston, CONNECTICUT

PHOTOGRAPHS BY SIMON UPTON

Perhaps it's the Caribbean-blue front door that announces that this is no ordinary bucolic retreat. Or maybe it's the life-sized plaster cow in the front yard, with one side painted with the Canadian flag and the other the Stars and Stripes. Or the giant fiberglass head of a Roman woman tucked under a Father Hugo rosebush. No matter where you turn, wit and whimsy continually dance with serenity and comfort at Susan Winberg and Ken Shewer's Connecticut weekend home they share with their children, Max and Zoe. Perched on a ridge overlooking Lake Waramaug, the butter-yellow 1840s Greek Revival house holds as many elegant surprises inside as it does out. But the house is also about comfort and offering repose to its busy family, who come most weekends to relax. "It has a calming effect, and always makes me smile," says Susan, who is an interior designer. Susan and Ken, who

opposite: In the sun room, the family wanted to bring the outside in, where birds and light abound. The large gold spheres used to be Christmas ornaments for a public space, and now bring a touch of magic to a private one.

opposite: In the dining room Winberg and artist Lyndon Andrews painted a mural on all four walls depicting the property in the early 1800s and then personalized it by adding family details.

have a passion for the bold and the eclectic, furnished most of the house with pieces from local artisans, antiques stores, and flea markets. Their artful juxtaposition of elements soothes as much as it stimulates.

When Winberg and Shewer found the property it was in pristine condition, but the gardens were in need of amplification. Beds were expanded and revitalized and used to link the many components of the property together, including the tennis court and pool house the couple added. Now there are as many as eight gardens, each unique but all connected through common plants and colors, as well as out-door sculptures.

It was almost two years before the couple began any interior design. First Susan, along with an artist friend from Toronto, painted over the bad floors in the living area and dining room with a handmade tool that gave them a unique combedlike texture.

Since the property used to be called Ash Grove, Ken had the idea to commemorate its history by creating a large ash flower and leaf stencil pattern throughout the entryway. The swirling effect feels like a Matisse painting blown out of its frame. In the dining room, Susan

**opposite:** In the kitchen pantry, Winberg painted the traditional stained oak floors stone white to contemporize the space. The walls were hand painted to resemble the look and feel of linen and then punctuated with wire-rimmed baskets found at a flea market.

**this page:** In the master bedroom, Winberg, along with artist Lyndon Andrews, stenciled the walls with a traditional American pattern but played up the scale for a more modern take.

painted all four walls to depict the surrounding area as it would have looked in the 1800s, and then personalized it with familial locations such as Zoe's horse barn and Max's boathouse. For the floors, she used a hand-made tool of corrugated cardboard to glaze and comb a custom pattern. As far as furnishings went, Susan and Ken's motto is simple: "If we love it, we'll find a place for it." A stuffed swan found at a nearby antiques shop lives upstairs, a life-sized emu can be found downstairs, and delicate dolls' heads decorate the fireplace mantel.

The family loves to eat outside on their screened-in porch. With its large-

opposite: In the screened-in porch, a picnic table top by York Street Studio is transformed with copper wrapped in wood planks and a bronze base. The red lacquer chairs give an unexpected twist on Shaker style.

this page: A fiberglass head found in an old opera house is now an integral part of the garden. "She is our own Greek goddess," says Winberg.

scale checkerboard floor, picnic-style table made out of copper and bronze, and red lacquer chairs, it offers a stylish perch from which to admire the undulating hills. And when this family isn't admiring their surroundings, they are biking, waterskiing, horseback riding, or simply reading. Such are seasonal pleasures in a community the family has come to cherish. "Since we don't live here every day," says Ken, "it's not in a state of chaos when we arrive. It's just waiting for us to enjoy it."

# RESURRECTED CHARM

Long Island, NEW YORK

PHOTOGRAPHS BY WILLIAM ABRANOWICZ

For some, it is as simple and serendipitous as seeing a real estate ad in a newspaper one weekday morning. By Sunday morning, interior and product designer Tricia Foley had driven out to Long Island to assess in person the 1845 shingle house that beckoned to her in print; she purchased it within the hour. It wasn't perfection that caught her eye, but rather imperfection: "As a designer who loves saving houses, this was a dream, to discover an old wreck with history and bring it back to life." With its bad 1960s wallpaper, paneling, vinyl flooring, and boarded-up fireplace, she had her work cut out for her. Luckily, Foley had an able makeover crew by her side: with five brothers, a handyman father, and lots of pizza, she and her family set off to work at a brisk pace. "We had many weekend construction parties," Foley remembers. All surfacing was stripped to find the "true bones" of the place, and soon Foley was able to layer on the architectural details where there had been none: dropped ceilings were removed to unveil old beams, which were then stripped and restored. New moldings were added to the windows, and period doors rescued from flea markets replaced existing ones throughout. Wall paneling was created around the fireplace to make it the natural focal point for cozy gath-

opposite: In Foley's bedroom an 1820s mahogany sleigh bed is flanked by a tree-trunk table decorated withquince branches and stones collected from walks on the beach.

opposite: Simple shelves on brackets create a more spacious look in the nineteenth-century house where space is limited. An island is fashioned out of an old aquarium stand and now serves as tabletop storage.

this page: In the dining area of the kitchen, the old farmhouse table is finished in glossy white. The shelving unit was bought from a catalog and also painted white to look like it had always been there. The dining chair is from Ikea.

opposite: Foley created a fireplace in the living room with raised wood panelling. The wide plank pine floor boards are whitewashed.

above: Tricia Foley sits in an eighteenth-century reproduction leather wing chair. A collection of old glass decanters are displayed on a painted table below a simply framed Agnes Martin print.

erings in a space that may be small on square footage (at just 1,000 square feet) but immense on charm and comfort.

With a living room, kitchen, bedroom, and bathroom downstairs and just a bedroom and tiny bath above, Foley created a sense of space by using different shades of white on the walls, floors, and shutters: "I wanted it to be clean, spare but not museumlike." She brought in furniture that echoed that philosophy: brown leather wing chairs in the living room are eighteenth-century reproductions, which Foley loves for their modern, simple lines. The large white sofa was a barn sale find that was promptly upholstered in comfortable white linen. "It really anchors the room," explains Foley. Wedgwood china and crystal collected on travels and local antiquing are displayed in stacks on the kitchen's open shelves.

But the hardest-working piece in the home is the white-painted farm table she found for $75 at a barn sale and recoats periodically: "I work at it, entertain on it, fold laundry there: it is the house's cornerstone." It also offers the best views to the outside porch (Foley tore down the dilapidated original and built this ideal warm-weather entertaining space in its place), and backyard. An herb garden Foley revived offers plenty of herbs to put in her dishes. But the real impetus to cook is to set her beloved white table and arrange it with flowers in preparation for company. As there is no driveway, guests pull right up onto the grass and park along the white picket fence. Weekends involve canoeing in the nearby lake, visiting farm stands, or poring through books on rainy days over pots of tea. "I love that it's so relaxing and easy here," says Foley. "It's a perfect place whether I am by myself for quiet time or welcoming friends."

# MAINE BY WAY OF BERLIN

Arrowsic, MAINE

PHOTOGRAPHS BY WILLIAM ABRANOWICZ

For most, a weekend retreat's value is its ability to deliver tranquility via a car or train. But sometimes the reward of the ideal destination is worth jumping on a plane, even a time zone or two. For this European couple and their young daughter, who live in Berlin, acquiring a seventeen-acre island in Maine was as alluring as if it were only a few steps away. They fell in love with the landscape while visiting during a study sojourn in the States, its craggy beauty reminding the father of his childhood in Sweden. And its exotic location didn't seem so distant considering the frequent business trips they made to New York. After reading about its availability in a German newspaper, they visited the island, which is connected to the mainland via a causeway near the Kennebec River. While mostly jungle and mosquitoes, the pull of magnificent possibility was strong enough that a few weeks later the property was theirs.

There was initially only a lonely 1890 farmhouse on the island, and the water could not even be seen due to the intense vegetation surrounding the house. But over the next twenty years, the owners cleared and constructed different houses on the property, doing everything themselves and turning the island into a community made

opposite: The terrace between the main glass house and cottage offers open air views of the lake beyond.

———

70

form hanging from the ceiling. The owners had seen this staircase in a magazine and relished the opportunity to duplicate it.

oppoite: In the cottage guest bedroom a selection of photography shares company with the owners' collection of old globes.

of wood, stone, and windows, with the shelters strung together by wooden walkways inspired by Maine's summer camps of the 1920s.

There are two main houses: one is used as the kitchen and social area, with three glass walls and one stone wall, maximizing views of the surrounding water. The second is the master bedroom, also comprised mainly of glass and views. The other two buildings serve as guest cottages, one a former Coast Guard building that was spotted roadside one day and then transported back to the island and remodeled to become the ideal relaxation nook.

Whether you are inside, out on a terrace, or down below on the floating dock, the idea is to admire and enjoy the magnificence of nature year-round. But there is much to entertain the eye inside as well: everywhere an international array of treasures is displayed with

opposite: The pitcher
and salt-and-pepper
shaker collection was
acquired by trips and
travels around the globe.

this page: In the kitchen,
an antique cabinet
from a local Maine work-
shop has been trans-
formed into a unique wet
bar and storage space.

opposite:
The outdoor sauna
and shower are
located close to the
shore of the
Kennebec River.

an artful, often humorous touch. "Being art dealers, we love to play with all the different ways to exhibit and present things we love, no matter what their monetary worth. This is our joy." An ashtray found on the couple's Cambodian honeymoon, a pair of stuffed albatross wings from London, and a vintage Mobil Oil steel Pegasus horse from a nearby antiques store are all testament to people who are as passionate about traveling as they are about coming home. Cooking is another love, especially when local ingredients offer such sumptuous classics like lobster salad, corn on the cob, and oysters with steak, always shared with friends and family who visit from around the world. And no matter where they are coming from, everyone feels a sense of instant relaxation as they begin to make their way toward the island: "Once we cross that causeway, we allow ourselves to find another rhythm, to be enveloped by nature."

78

# CONTEMPORARY BARN

Stanfordville, NEW YORK

PHOTOGRAPHS BY JOHN GRUEN

It is not often that weekend retreats are born from drawings on café napkins in Paris, but in the case of the van der Geests, necessity was the mother of invention. "We always had a dream to have a country place where we could entertain, live, and play with all the ease we could think of," explains Eduard, who is Dutch, of he and his wife, Selina, who is English. So a few years later and over three thousand miles away in Hudson Valley, New York, the sketch of dreams became a reality: a symmetrical barnlike contemporary home, fashioned from vintage silver gray barn siding, along with twelve-foot-square oak hand-hewn beams. Surrounded by woodland and abundant wildlife, it sits at the end of a winding dirt drive, past ponds and fields. One enters directly into the mudroom, which feels like the ultimate way station between outdoor and indoor pleasure. There is reassuring order here, with symmetrical closets set with wire meshing (built by Eduard), but also fancifulness, as in the vintage frames (collected by Selina) hung alongside hunting trophies. A pair of Chinese barn doors grandly gives way to the great room, the heart and soul of the home, which, despite its soaring twenty-eight-foot ceilings, still embraces you with a peaceful hospitality that is part French country, part Zen.

opposite: The great room features a Louis XIII stone mantelpiece that was bought in France before the house was built.

this page:The main house was built from recycled barn siding and sits in a field surrounded by woods and ponds at the end of a half-mile long driveway.

opposite: The granite mudroom floor was shipped from Belgium. Eduard made the closets, above which hang some of Selina's frame collection.

At one end is the living area, punctuated by a great fireplace complete with seventeenth-century soapstone mantel. (It took six months to get an export passport so that it could leave France.) In full view at the other end is a serene Swedish-style kitchen, where Selina elegantly displays glass jars full of tempting goodies and Eduard whips up much-anticipated breakfasts featuring blue eggs from nearby farms. When it's time to eat, European and local guests congregate around

82

opposite: In the kitchen, concrete counters and backsplash pair well with Ikea cabinets Selina painted white. Antique baking molds are artfully arranged above the stove.

this page: In the master bedroom, the closet features nineteenth century Chinese screen doors, and a feathered headdress from Africa hangs above the bed.

opposite: The drinks cabinet is part of Selina's steel furniture collection and was a birthday gift for Eduard. Above hang some of their collection of European drawings.

the enormous fourteenth-century country table at the center of the room. Selina, an accomplished decorator, acted as her own general contractor and designer, and knows a thing or two about solving problems with personal panache. When a suitable drinks cabinet could not be found, for example, she simply fashioned one of her own design out of steel. When budget dictated Ikea cabinets for the kitchen, she had them sanded and painted to achieve just the dove-gray patina she wanted.

Whether reclining fireside or helping with the culinary preparations, visitors are surrounded by Eduard and Selina's intimate displays of beloved objects brought back from their travels the world over. From the nineteenth-century watercolors dotting the living room landscape, to the Chinese wooden screens in the master shower, to a Belgian white cupboard in the kitchen, guests are encouraged to get close, admire, and, always, touch.

With the new addition of a pool just steps from the house (complete with outdoor stained oak furniture designed by Selina), the house is an even greater destination for friends from both England and Holland. Visits to the local farmer's market are a weekend ritual, as is walking with Zola, the couple's Welsh springer. In the winter Selina is in charge of snow blowing, and in the summer she mows the lawns (she says it's the ultimate therapy), while Eduard busies himself with the constant attention such an active household requires. The van der Geests' most important task each day is to create the ideal environment for themselves and those they cherish. Says Selina, "We want our house guests to feel they are somewhere special."

# OPEN DOOR POLICY

Copake Lake, NEW YORK

PHOTOGRAPHS BY MICHAEL MUNDY

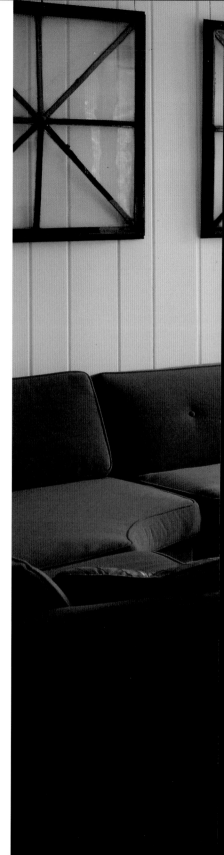

"Everyone told us not to buy it," says designer Chase Booth of the retreat he and his partner, Gray Davis, now own on Copake Lake at the foothills of the Berkshires. "Our parents, our lawyer, the home inspector, even our real estate agent." Having been abandoned for the past eight years, the property was completely overgrown and vandals had buzz-sawed off sections of the knotty pine paneling—not to mention that the ceilings had collapsed and there was no front door. Its shape, however, was perfection. "Like a picture of a house a child would draw with its four sides and gabled roof," recalls Booth. Lovesick with the house's possibilities, he and Davis were undeterred by its detractors. "The house just wanted to be happy and have people in it." The first order of business was to move the 1,700-square-foot cottage to its ideal loca-

opposite: A '60s acid-green sofa picked up from an estate sale and white pleather chairs are grounded by a luxe Algerian goat-skin rug purchased in Paris.

88

this page: Spare pine
siding painted white
combined with simple
pendant light fixtures
from Ikea set a serene
tone for dining. Ebony
floors give the rougher
edges of the old cabin
sophistication.

opposite: Keeping a
neutral palette through-
out, the vintage side-
board, black- and-white
photographs, and a
Polish movie poster are
all part of the casual
ease of the room. The
sideboard also doubles
as a bar.

opposite: Vintage sports equipment add a bit of levity to a Robjohns-Gibbings chair.

tion thirty feet closer to the lake and angle it for the most efficient sun exposure. They completely winterized the structure, the old kitchen was torn out and moved to the front of the house to open up views of the lake, and wood floors were laid down in all the living areas and tiles installed in the bathrooms. In addition, a row of French doors brightened the lake side of the house and decks on the front and back of the structure increased entertainment and lounging space. Once the walls were sprayed a glossy white and its floors ebonized, "Poof! A brand new house from an old shell was born!" says Davis.

Davis is an accomplished designer and Booth a set producer with a flair of his own, so décor proved to be a snap. "We were on a tight budget and had to be creative," says Booth. They pillaged estate sales, auctions, and junk stores to ultimately outfit the cottage so that it is both modern and eclectic but, most importantly, "a place where nothing is so precious that a wet bathing suit can't be plunked down on it." An acid-green sofa, white patent leather chairs, and black-framed art all punch up the neutral palette, and subtle lighting tones down any imperfections. Now the living, dining, and kitchen area is all essentially one room that acts as a kind of giant pool house, with barriers between water and shelter blissfully removed. "Sometimes people are put out by the vast numbers of birds and bugs flying through the house," says Davis. But the more the merrier as far as these consummately unpretentious hosts are concerned. A steady stream of friends and neighbors, children and dogs, know the way to their door and that

it is always open. Since they never cook in the city, all meals here are eaten at home, with fifteen the average head count. "It's a great mix of families, local and city folk: a true melting pot," says Chase, who often serves his Indian or Mexican specialties of the house.

The lake brings year-round pleasure: drifting in their neighbor's pontoon boat with friends and cocktails for hours in the warmer months, and on top of giant ottomans enjoying bonfires in the winter. "Listening to the ice shift is haunting and truly beautiful," says Davis. And how about all those naysayers: aren't they glad they didn't listen to them? Smiles Chase, "They could kick themselves now."

# MEMORY GARDEN

PHOTOGRAPHS BY MICHAEL PARTENIO

"I really think the door to a house should be important, no matter the style or size," believes interior designer Philip Gorrivan. So when it came to outfitting the door on the white-picketed Connecticut retreat where he, his wife, Lisa, and their two young children spend nearly every weekend year-round, it had to be one of both style and substance. Now, a custom mahogany door greets the steady stream of house guests who flock to this tiny 1880 cottage knowing that across its threshold an abundant welcome always awaits.

The Gorrivans purchased the home from a woman who had lived there for almost a hundred years. The 1,600-square-foot house had been half the size when the woman moved in, the Lilliputian rooms eventually enlarged in the 1940s. And while Lisa and Phil knew they had to do extensive updates (kitchen and bathrooms), they didn't touch the original footprint of the house, nor the windows. "We wanted to restore, and not alter," says Lisa.

The floors were painted pale grays and French blues to cheer up the existing hardwood. Crown moldings were created to give definition, and barn board from the property was added to the children's room walls and painted white to give a rustic, permanent element.

opposite: The Gorrivans looked to the outside gardens for color inspiration in the living room.

97

this page: The guest room features a wonderful red and white vintage chinoi-serie alongside an 1830s console and a nineteenth-century Kashan that adds the perfect balance.

opposite: The Finnish chest was chosen for its unique color from a local antiques dealer. The pitchers belonged to Lisa's grandmother. The nineteenth-century caned chair is from Philip's childhood home in Portland, Maine.

opposte: A spot for a
quick escape: a nine-
teenth-century bergère
in vintage chinoiserie
is punctuated with a
beaded English toaster
cover transformed
into a pillow.

A nascent designer at the time, Philip was soon ready to cut his teeth on one of his first decorating projects. He was an easy first client: he knew he wanted to keep things simple and mostly traditional, layering in family treasures and cherished collections to personalize each room. "We wanted to come here and be surrounded by everything we love," he explains.

With innate aplomb, he hung nineteenth-century European old master drawings next to local artists and combined an eighteenth-century Dutch American cabinet with a maritime painting found at a garage sale (it reminded him of his Maine childhood). A tole lamp from the 1940s is equally at home next to a nineteenth-century Windsor chair.

Philip next tackled the landscaping, which needed extensive work. Luckily, gardening is his weekend passion, and he immediately set out to ultimately create twelve unique gardens on the property, all of them with different plant material and each identified by their own names and descriptions. Now five-year-old Charlie and eight-year-old Isabelle can choose from a bevy of magical places in which to frolic: the white, peony, or lily gardens, for example. Or they can remember their late grandmother by enjoying the yellow tulips planted in her name in the tulip garden, or visit the red swamp maple or the magnolia tree planted in their honor.

A patio was laid from stone native to the property and is the ideal stage for summer dinner parties. The Gorrivans like to cover a long table with linen and their cherished famille-verte china, and of course freshly cut flowers abound. In the winter, there is cross-country skiing and sledding behind the property and lots of cozy dinners inside, resplendent with friends and wine, often ending in the house specialty: tarte tatin. And those guests lucky enough to be sleeping over often awake in the morning to Charlie, who always has a question or two along with a smile encouraging them to greet the new day. This is surely a place where small feels big in the coziest of ways.

above: Isabelle and
Charlie and their
standard poodle, Clovis,
hurry down the
stone steps to get
to the meadow and
gardens beyond.

# LAKE COTTAGE

New Preston, CONNECTICUT

PHOTOGRAPHS BY DON FREEMAN

Perched on a rocky bluff overlooking Lake Waramaug is the ideal Connecticut retreat for a single weekender looking for great water views and the chance to take out his 1960s Chris Craft Super Sport any chance he gets. But before pleasure came many months of work restoring the dilapidated 1937 cottage that, over years, had been rented to the ground. "My parents have a cottage on the lake and I fell in love with the area," says the owner, venture capitalist Mark Adams. "When this place came up for sale it had aluminum siding, shag carpeting, and was sagging in the middle." But with its dramatic location, set in a hollow and surrounded by towering stone formations, Adams knew he could provide every room with its own water view.

While the bones of the house (along with the original wood flooring in the living room) were kept intact, every other element had to

opposite: The front porch is filled with vintage rattan furniture that once belonged to Adams's grandmother and now have been restored with care.

opposite: The dining room corner banquette is the ideal way to stylishly seat many guests for meals.

this page: The full-service kitchen is made cheeky with cabinet interiors painted apple green.

be meticulously rebuilt and restored. Adams brought designer Gil Shaefer in to help him and an architect who specialized in historic renovations. "I wanted it to feel eclectic but with an eye toward tradition," says Adams. To achieve just the right touch, he mixed family heirlooms and vintage pieces from Paris flea markets with more contemporary pieces to give the seven rooms a fresh edge. Guests watch the sunsets, gathered around the French farmhouse table on chic aluminum Hudson chairs in the dining room. For the screened-in porch, Adams revived his grandmother's beloved McGuire rattan furniture by painting it white and then covering it with plush pillows. His favorite room is the upstairs main guest room, which boldly boasts pink walls and green floors. "Every lake cottage should have one pink and green room," he says. A 1920s caned lounger would be the ideal repose for Sister Parish, who would feel equally at home in the children's guest

this page: An upstairs children's bedroom features beds covered in antique Indian madras quilts and vintage tennis racquets for wall décor.

opposite: The coveted outdoor shower offers privacy via moss-covered boulders and natural flora.

room (for Adams's nieces and nephews), with its madras bedspreads and vintage wooden tennis racquets (rescued from the garbage at his Manhattan digs) perched above one of the headboards. Visitors and host enjoy views no matter where they are in the house due to the three sets of French doors Adams installed across from one another in the front and back of the house. Besides sunrises and sunsets, Adams likes to entertain his frequent guests with steak barbecues, trips to nearby county fairs, and waterskiing on the lake. And upon return to the now cottage-cozy retreat, he has only one house rule: "Take off your shoes and stay barefoot all weekend."

# NEWPORT GLAMOUR

Newport, RHODE ISLAND

PHOTOGRAPHS BY JAMES MERRELL

**D**riving along this rugged isthmus, visitors may feel they're arriving in rural Maine and not Newport, Rhode Island, known for its trimmed hedges and jaunty yachts. But it is precisely its remote location, far from the crowds in town, that convinced San Francisco–based Tracey Roberts and her husband, Paul Haigney, to make Waterlot their summer house.

At the turn of the century, photographer Ernest Walter Histed built the turreted Waterlot as a backdrop for society portraits of the grand dames who lived down on Belleview Avenue. Cognizant of how the island posed unique renovation challenges—from its location to its meticulous Conservation Society—Roberts knew better than to change the footprint of Waterlot, and rather set to transform the rooms through paint, design juxtaposition, and visual trickery. "I envisioned

an elegant family beach house: something that reflected the glamour of Newport but that was also practical and modern," she says.

"Everything was crumbling," remembers Roberts. "The plumbing and wiring hadn't been tended to since the '30s." And the house's layout had been built to suit a working bachelor: ample entertaining space on the ground floor but a tiny kitchen, and no bathrooms upstairs. Roberts was able to solve these problems—many of them in her

opposite: Sophie on her pony in the formal gardens on the ocean side of Waterlot.

opposite: The downstairs living room is the family's favorite place to entertain. The tufted chairs and sofa are allegedly from Coco Chanel's shop in Paris and the blue lamps were found at a local antique shop. The trumeau above the fire mantel was purchased from Butterfield's and attributed to Boucher.

this page: The bamboo cabinet is from Ed Hardy in San Francisco and the shells are from a shop in Monterey. The antique nautilus spoon warmers were bought from Suzanne Rheinstein's Los Angeles shop Hollyhock, where Tracey got her design training and still loves to shop.

opposite: In the upstairs living room, Tracey up-holstered the curtains and chair in her all-time favorite shell pattern from Grey Watkins, La Glorie de la Mer.

above: Coco, the family's Cavalier King Charles spaniel, gets cozy in the house's original kitchen, which Tracey gave punch to by hanging the Shanghai Tang table lamps upside down, painting the cabinets green, and installing a cork floor.

dreams, her favorite workspace. And what she saw out her window when she awoke also helped: "Much of my inspiration came from the surrounding sea and landscape."

She made the entry hall glamorous by painting its walls Pratt & Lambert's aqua blue; a faux fireplace with a Sylvian Levy-Alban mantel creates a focal point, and a zebra rug on the black-and-white checkerboard floor adds instant dash. Antique Chinese-red lamps dangle from the ceiling like exotic earrings, the perfect accessories to the tulip-red front door.

The enormous living room offers resplendent cove and garden views. "I wanted the eye to go outside, as there is so much beauty there," says Roberts. Neutral but rich colors on the walls and curtains set the stage for the old and new pieces collected on Roberts's travels: tufted coral chairs reputedly from Coco Chanel's salon enjoy proximity with twin tangerine-orange Chris Spitzmiller lamps, and a mahogany game table circa 1820 grounds a scarlet Charles Edwards lantern overhead.

Upstairs, a sunroom addition has been revved up: the floor, once a fake white brick, is now covered in cork, and the walls are painted a pale green. Chairs were re-covered with Cowtan and Tout's coral leopard cotton, and étagères purchased locally define the room's corners. Guests gather round the French country table to feast on lobster, corn salsa, and berry pie baked with twelve-year-old Sophie.

Outside, Roberts, with the help of San Francisco–based landscape designer Andrea Cochran, fashioned a European garden that would create a sense of arrival for guests driving up to the house. Cochran's sensibility tends to the modern, but she and Roberts "share the same pruned, spatial approach," recalls Cochran, who says they worked well together. They transformed an undefined lawn into outdoor rooms bordered with old New England wall stones that help buffet

the strong winds and extend the house's architectural detail. Formal, parterre gardens of boxwood and lavender create a geometric silver and green pattern. A romantic cutting garden with David Austen roses softens the stern edges.

Roberts and her family enjoy antiquing in town, navigating the waters in kayaks, and roasting marshmallows over a bonfire. Roberts imagines that her grandchildren will one day play hide-and-seek among the rocky paths just as her children, Sophie, Myles, and Max, do now. "One moment we're building sand castles and the next we're hosting a sit-down dinner for ten. It's truly a magical place."

# PRIVATE GETAWAY

Unionville, PENNSYLVANIA

PHOTOGRAPHS BY WILLIAM ABRANOWICZ

Kevin Roberts had never been an equestrian before, but he soon realized that the only real way to get to know the Chester County countryside where he had purchased a weekend retreat was on horseback, as its most glorious parts were inaccessible by car. Now, many lessons later, riding boots are a permanent part of the décor at his eighteenth-century Pennsylvania home.

Enthusiasm and respect for both the historical and natural elements of his surroundings were equally in evidence when he set out to restore the property he purchased in 1987 from a couple who divorced before renovations began. So Roberts, along with his partner, Timothy Haynes (they helm the celebrated interior design firm Haynes-Roberts), embraced the property's deplorable condition with the confidence of knowing that the deteriorating house, with its leaky roofs and lack of heat and electricity, could someday be transformed into a humble estate with magnificent charm.

There are three buildings on the property: the main house, a guest house, and a barn, which serves as both garage and entertaining space. The main house, originally built to accommodate mill workers for an adjacent mill, was lodged in the side of a hill, so Roberts pushed

opposite: In the kitchen, a plaster bust of Mrs. Pennypacker, wife of the governor of Pennsylvania from 1903–1907 is used here as a hat rack.

this page: The guest house sits directly across the road from the main house on the Brandy `wine River. Originally built in the late eighteenth century as an oyster house, it was later used as a one-room schoolhouse.

opposite: The interior of the barn, which is now used as the summer living room. This barn was brought to the property and constructed adjacent to the main house so that one can pass from the library directly in.

opposite: In the eating area of the kitchen, an eighteenth-century Pennsylvania scrub-top tripod pine table is surrounded by French metal folding chairs.

it back to create gardens and terraces from ancient local brick and stone walls. Inside, Roberts was equally creative: he turned five of the small mill-worker bedrooms into a large music room, complete with beautiful balcony and primitive stairway. When guests aren't enjoying themselves there, they can retire to the guest quarters, formerly an old schoolhouse that Roberts painstakingly returned to its original, double-heighted configuration. A barn was transplanted from nearby and serves as a garage downstairs, and as a large entertaining area upstairs that connects to the main house through the library. When it finally came time to decorate, Roberts chose to embrace the house's roots, but in a spare and quirky style. "There was so much beauty in the original space that I decided to defer to the architecture." He left all the peeling beams exposed to celebrate their wonderful patina and restored the house's details using only locally found antique hardware and glass. Where original floors were missing, Roberts replaced them with eighteenth-century attic boards from nearby farms. "I didn't want the house to look like a historical re-creation." And because these

opposite: At the front door, an overscaled iron bucket is now cleverly used for boots.

this page: In the library, an early nineteenth-century Vermont handwoven cotton rug was made by joining five 25-inch- wide runners. The chaise was a metamorphic campaign bed from the early 19th century, and an antique drill band drum now acts as an end table.

original farmhouses contained much less furniture than is used today, Roberts kept his rooms spare. Still, whimsy and sophistication abound in all the right places: an over-sized chess set found in London awaits challenge, a pair of oversized plaster busts stand guard in the kitchen window sills and act as hat racks. A small cupboard in the living room is fashioned out of orange crates.

Roberts loves to cook seasonal, local fare for family and friends: picnics are an especially treasured occasion, and hampers of home-made food are spread out on a woodland clearing above the house that offers spectacular views of the Brandywine River. Guests, however, are less apt to cross the threshold than the sound of Roberts's boots as he comes in from riding or gardening. He admits, "I really like to keep this place as a private getaway for myself."

# REFINED FARMHOUSE

Washington Depot, CONNECTICUT

PHOTOGRAPHS BY JOHN GRUEN

"The great thing about this property is that you have no idea what to expect when you first turn in the driveway," says owner and interior designer Susan Bednar Long of the Connecticut retreat she and her husband, John, and their two-year-old son, Baker, visit every weekend.

A small, unmarked gravel driveway reveals none of the treasures that await visitors: an 1800s farmhouse flanked on one side by orchards of apple, pear, and peach trees and a stream and old stone walls on the other.

When they first discovered the property four years ago, the house was a mixture of Southwest style and antique farmhouse. The Longs loved how the previous owners had added skylights to the beamed-ceiling rooms to create airy spaces. But since Sue and John leaned

opposite: The dining room is in the old part of the late 1800s farmhouse. The chrome modern bench, which Long upholstered in indestructible faux ostrich leather, is her young son's favorite place to eat.

125

126

this page: Long transformed a twentieth-century Danish Modern sofa by re-covering it in silk damask and the banquette seat cushion in cotton velvet. It's low back and long length provide a visual break between the start of the living room seating area and the entry area behind it.

opposite: The sterling silver pieces on the mantel are part of a collection that the Longs display and use throughout the house. The small bowls are baby bowls owned by John's ancestor, John Roach. The flower plate is from Buccellati.

opposite: In the living room, the raw silk draperies are hung on iron rods about 15 inches higher than the window and door frames to accentuate the high ceilings and give the appearance of grander openings.

toward a more tailored, masculine décor, some changes were immediately made to define the house's tone. They stained the wood beams darker, removed shag carpeting to reveal handsome wide-plank pine floors, added recessed lighting in the living room and kitchen, and transformed the stair railings to a more refined spindle, to name just a few. The subtle but decisive improvements set the stage for a sophistication that can be both functional and playful. As president of the New York design firm Tocar, Sue knew immediately how she wanted to decorate: "I am in love with Bill Blass's former country house nearby and

this page: Antique oval
mirrors have been
thoughtfully arranged
on the open wall to
add sculptural interest
to this airy space, as
well as reflect the view
from the windows
opposite.

oppersite: Susan and
John bought as a
wedding present
to each other the
two silver-leaf-
framed shell prints in
Florence, Italy, a few
days before getting
married in Venice.

how he celebrated neutrals." The Longs' living room now pays perfect homage, with its creams and mahogany textures and hues. A Danish Modern sofa, which Sue found at a local garage sale, was given new life with silk damask and cotton velvet. Poised between the den and living room, a chrome and glass bar cart twinkles for guests at night. Nine antique oval convex mirrors line the upstairs hallway, each with a slightly different frame. The master bedroom has a more European flavor, punctuated by pieces Sue sparked to on her travels and brought home to roost: a very large Bavarian antler chandelier, antique Italian ceramic lamps, and a cut-out leather headboard reminiscent of the one she and John saw while in Venice for their wedding.

A third-floor, cornflower blue–striped office acts as Sue's retreat within a retreat: "I wanted the space to remind me of a beachfront room along the Amalfi Coast, albeit one with a New England spirit."

Outside, a hideaway of another sort awaits: Lemonade Lake, a private fifty-acre lake built by neighbors in the 1950s offers ideal fly-fishing in the summer and ice skating the winter. And every season the gardens and foliage surrounding the Longs' property offer a bevy of centerpiece opportunities for dinner parties. "Baker loves to yell, 'Clippers, clippers!' and we are off to find something new to cut and bring inside," says John. And whenever he and Sue reenter, their feelings for what has grown both in and around their house blooms as if for the first time. "We believe in keeping everything visually beautiful so that every time we arrive we think, 'I love this house!'"

above: The trellis at
the front gate to the
vegetable and herb
garden is covered
with a large climbing
hydrangea bush.

# EASY MANOR

Washington, CONNECTICUT

PHOTOGRAPHS BY MIKI DUISTERHOF

They first saw their weekend retreat online. The only pictures in the listing had been taken at night; it was a large house, perched atop a hill surrounded by forest and misty tree lines. "It looked like a haunted French manor house," remembers actress Sophie Drubner, "with that great faded grandeur that reminded me of how our grandparents lived." She and her husband, Jeff, were instantly smitten. "We had to occupy those spooky rooms!"

As they drove up for their first look, past the mature pear trees and around the circular drive at the top of the hill, with its Japanese maple and stone garden, the now sun-drenched house looked downright cheerful. But the Drubners were still enchanted: "It had that old-school restraint that is harder and harder to find," says Jeff, who admits they would have taken the house in any condition but were

lucky that the previous owners had kept it well maintained. But improvements were made in both the humbling and alluring categories: the Drubners shingled the house for a more cottage-y touch and added a pool and tennis court to glam up the landscape.

As far as decorating the vast rooms with their high ceilings, Sophie knew she needed to create a mood that was both masculine and simple

opposite: In the mudroom a Sumatra basket holds polo mallets and an old family riding helmet. On the console is a still life of petrified mushrooms, antlers, old iron tools, and an eighteenth-century skeleton key found on the property.

134

opposite: In the living room neutral couches provide the perfect backdrop for Middle Eastern furniture, rugs, and textile designs. The abstract expressionist painting is by Philip Wofford, circa 1960. The coffee table was bought at a bazaar in Tunis.

this page: In Olivia's room, the walls were hand painted in a stencil of medieval European townsfolk in the style of Ludwig Bemelmans. The shelves are filled with a collection of vintage toys mixed with the children's books and their own artworks. The ladder leads to a loft with twin beds.

to keep the spaces feeling grounded. So going on part instinct, part trial and error, and part feng shui, she began to mix all the eclectic pieces of furniture, art, and collectibles that she and Jeff had amassed over the years. "We like to put the eccentric, the simple, and the grand next to one another in conventional groupings, knowing that the colors already work well together," explains Sophie. Truman Capote's teapots (won at Joanna Carson's auction) sit below a Philip Wofford abstract painting, and old Moroccan end tables provide the ideal place to put exotic drinks. "Classical ease is what we're aiming for," Jeff says.

Their favorite room is the dining room, which, tucked at one end

of the house, feels more like an elegant retreat than a social hub. "It's so far above the ground, people feel like they're on a ship at high seas," says Sophie, who counterbalanced the plentitude of light streaming in with a dark wood dining table, old English boardroom chairs, and an antique Turkoman carpet. Here guests are treated to a variety of seasonal and cultural dishes, as the Drubners love to entertain and serve exotic fare that echoes their passion for travel, from India to Italy. Through the room's tall windows that face east, south, and west, Hank, their beloved Smoushond, can be seen making his brisk rounds of the property in hopes of encountering a wild turkey or deer. The entire family loves to be outside year round. In the winter, it's for cross-country skiing or sledding. When it's warm, the pool is the focus, and its simple, elegant lines make laps a pleasure. Sophie and her eight-year-old daughter, Olivia, planted lavender, succulents, and wild grasses along one end of the pool so that "if you squint you can pretend you're in the South of France." Except that there is no need to wish oneself elsewhere. Says Jeff: "This house isn't just a refuge but a venue to explore things we love to do."

# CABANA
# CHIC

PHOTOGRAPHS BY GEOFF SPEAR

opposite: The pool house, built in the early 60s, is a short walk from the main house and overlooks acres of parklike property and the Litchfield hills beyond.

W hen they moved from one weekend retreat to another, it wasn't just an opportunity to change locations (even though they were going just two bucolic Connecticut towns over), it was a chance for Bruce Glickman and Wilson Henley, owners of a Manhattan furniture shop, Duane, to decorate in a completely new design style. They said good bye to the 1740s antiques-filled farmhouse and hello to a 1954 Modernist ranch with glass walls. "We went from a cozy cottage in the Cotswolds to a James Bond movie," says Bruce.

That meant that many vintage pieces from their former abode, like the nineteenth-century French commode and the beloved "dog lady" portrait from Henley's family, no longer fit their new house's posh personality. But Bruce and Wilson weren't about to host an estate sale: they were too fond of all they had gathered over years of passionate

opposite: After painting
everything in high
gloss white, Glickman
and Henley created
an eclectic décor with
the best "leftovers" from
their prior residence.

traveling and collecting. So they gave much of the cherished furniture from the old house fresh life inside the new property's hot spot:
the pool house. In a setting fit for a Slim Aarons shoot, the spacious
bungalow overlooks the bright blue fifty-foot pool that architecturally
complements the main house as seamlessly as an olive does a martini.

Inside, however, the décor stands its own stylistic ground, eschew-
ing all things modern and edgy. At once a guest cottage, changing
cabana, and party pad, the pool house is now a temple to relaxation,
as long as it's done with style. Here, the miniature rooms echo the
relaxed sophistication of their former grown-up home, but with a
nod toward their playful new setting. A Jens Risom chest adds just
the right touch of formality to the elegant changing room, complete
with beach towels and extra bathing suits, while a red lacquered Karl
Springer console and Louis-style bergères covered in cowhide give
the main room cozy dash. Here inside the living and sleeping quarters is the perfect perch to admire the ten-acre property that spreads

HERB RITTS WORK

ALLURE    DIANA VREELAND    DOUBLEDAY

DENNIS HOPPER 1712 NORTH CRESCENT HEIGHTS

Alessi    Michael Collins    CARBON

garden junk    Mary Randolph Carter

KAREN BLIXEN'S FLOWERS

MAWSON    Kentucky Bluegrass    University of Kentucky Art Museum

The Garden Room

Antique Garden Ornament    Barbara Israel

The Last Country Houses    Yale

The English Country Cottage    Christopher    FRIEDMAN/EAIDEAS

EDGAR DEGAS, Photographer    The Metropolitan Museum of Art

classic modern    midcentury modern at home

Essential    FRANK LLOYD WRIGHT

LANDMARKS of Bridge

American Farmh

PEGGY GUGGENHEIM

Dickey/Felber    Insid

MACKESWOLD • ELEANOR WEILER
THE GOLDEN AGE of AMER
Pound Deserts | Private Estates

THE CUTTING EDGE    EDITED

e Finest Houses of Paris

Zona Home

AT HOME

luxuriously out past the balcony or to the pool below without getting wet. If houseguests need to brew coffee or their hosts need to prepare hors d'oeuvres, an open, white kitchen stretches neatly off to the side. Whether used as a breakfast nook, gossip cave, or reclusive retreat, the entire space serves to restore and rejuvenate. "Everyone wants to stay here," says Wilson, "including us!" Contentment is year-round: the rooms are heated in the winter and in the summer, much of Bruce and Wilson's entertaining centers around the deck that hovers glamorously over the pool. Here they grill and have cocktails with their abundant circle of friends, and late-night dips are often preferred over dessert. And sometimes, the only entertainment needed is a glorious outdoor shower with its expansive view of hills and sky. "Life here" says Bruce, "is a constant treat."

145

# OCTAGONAL
# INSPIRATION

Clermont, NEW YORK

PHOTOGRAPHS BY PHIL MANSFIELD

When Mike Gladstone dreamed of a weekend retreat, it was always the same vision he'd had since he was a teenager, when he first saw Monticello and was captivated by the idea of octagonal rooms and the possibilities of walls blending into one another. "It's a great revelation, thinking about space instead of boundaries," says Gladstone, a publishing consultant. Over the years he visited many variations on this theme and was captivated by the distinct light that vaulted ceilings would allow when they were topped by a cupola: "It just never ceased to intrigue me." He also knew that realizing such an endeavor would be costly. So when a friend offered him a three-acre building site on her eighty-three-acre estate east of the Hudson River, Gladstone knew he had to muster as much innovation as imagination to make his octagonal dream come true.

**147**

Luckily, a close friend, New York architect Michael Altschuler (who weekends in nearby Churchtown), stepped into the equation and became the ideal collaborator. "We both share similar passions for space, light, details, and the careful use of money," says Altschuler, who found a cost-effective solution to his client's predicament when he spotted a modular grain bin on a nearby farm and encouraged Gladstone to crawl into it with him. Both were impressed by the potential quality of the light. Before long, Gladstone's site contained a 450-square-foot octagonal living and bedroom space rising inside a sheet-metal cylinder—at half the previously estimated cost. A nineteen-foot-high domed ceiling topped with an oculus continues to delight Gladstone with its ability to diffuse light. "Being there is like being in a chapel because it is so responsive to the subtlest changes in natural light," he says.

As far as furnishing his new, open space for himself and Andy, his aging but still active border terrier, he approached the job "alone but with a few persuasive critics," in a style he refers to as "twentieth-century cumulative, with everything more or less a favorite." The effect is both minimal and personal, with a utilitarian intent. Flatware is stored in mustard crocks on open shelves so it can be viewed along with the art and found objects Gladstone displays for daily appreciation. Many of the treasures bring personal memories with their lineage: a seventeenth-century Italian altarpiece found in Massachusetts in the 1940s frames the mirror over the kitchen sink, and a Frank Gehry corrugated cardboard table in the living room is "a late Bloomingdale's markdown that caught my eye as I came down the escalator in the 1950s." Aalto stools that have been plant stands in his parents' 1960s house near Washington offer extra seating, along with some Bertoia chairs that were cast-offs from the Museum of Modern Art garden when Gladstone worked next door. Paintings and sculpture by artist neighbors are displayed alongside early-nineteenth-century portraits and Japanese Westernization prints.

The house's surrounding landscape "owes a lot to Downing," says

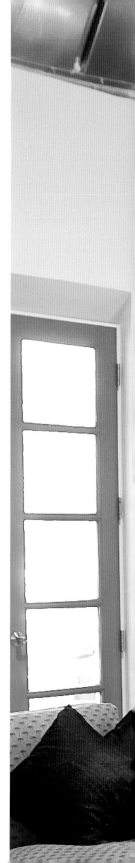

opposite: In the kitchen the clerestory light comes down in shafts, making a tight space feel airy.

this page: An Italian altarpiece from a Maine church offers ample reflection to cooks and guests alike.

Gladstone, who likes to keep his little part of it as "naturalistic" as possible. "Clearing"—as the house is aptly named due to the cleared foundation site—sits at the edge of a mile-long driveway on an otherwise wooded rise.

Weekends now bring quiet, productive work, which tends to echo Gladstone's weekday activities in the city—reading and "coping with the computer." For diversion, local haunts offer much good food, films, and music. When it's time for Andy's daily exercise, Gladstone, who walks with some difficulty, makes unusual use of the luxuriously long driveway: as he spots native plants and wild mushrooms from behind the wheel of the car, Andy happily lopes alongside until it's time to turn around and head home for dinner.

# UNITED BLISS

Accord, NEW YORK

PHOTOGRAPHS BY DAVE ENGELHARDT

"Every week we are discovering new things that need repair or restoring," say magazine directors Rina and Brittain Stone of their weekend retreat in Accord, New York. But the 1749 stone house on fifteen acres is beloved by its caretakers nonetheless. So much so that they hosted their wedding reception there, complete with a horse-drawn wagon delivering the newlyweds to their guests and seating cards dangling from tree branches. In fact it was the magic of the old trees, the strong light, and the parklike setting that charmed them several years ago and inspired them to end their house hunt after spotting the property via a realty Web site they were addicted to perusing. Search finally over, they set out to rework some shoddy 1980s renovation. The kitchen had to be transformed from a tiny U-shaped space with little counter

opposite: In the den, a deer loaned from old friends who moved to France but later got divorced, now stands guard over weekend activities. The yellow paint was chosen to work best with the bright light and Danish furniture.

this page: Assorted boots wait to conquer whatever weather and activity the day brings.

opposite: The front entrance has classic Dutch transom windows that bring in a great deal of light, making it a perfect place to loiter and welcome guests.

opposite: In a guest
bedroom, the deep
windows angle the
light for a Vermeer
effect, and the walls
are kept deliberately
spartan.

space to a galley layout with a big farm sink that is open to the great
room so that cooks can be part of the dinner party. Upstairs, a giant
sleeping loft was made into a proper master bedroom and bath, and
floors were treated with tung oil to give them a rich, subdued finish.
Besides that, it was a lot of "patch and paint," says Brittain. Walls were
painted thoughtfully, with many of the colors echoing the gray hues
of the stones used in the house.

The décor is also still a work in progress, which the Stones are tack-
ling themselves in a style they term "eclectic with a bit of taxidermy."
On the eclectic side, furniture and accessories have colorful histories:
an antique map featuring Accord and found by a friend gives official
welcome in the front hall; a French country hutch, having been cast
out by another friend's fiancé, was adopted and now serves as bar. A
stuffed pheasant and two deer find a home in the almost-black library,
the ideal haven for cigars and gentlemanly secrets.

Outside, neighbors pitched in to uncover and recover a trove of
landscape treasures: one found an elaborate walking garden of ferns,
peonies, and lily of the valley, while another repaired all the stone
benches and bird baths along the path. Brittain has meanwhile moved
walking paths into the overgrown fields behind the barn, leaving a
spectacular show of goldenrod, Queen Anne's lace, and winter berry.

Despite two years of lots of sawdust and lack of furniture, guests still
happily flock to visit and feel right at home. "People naturally connect

this page: Clippings from the outdoors are often Rina and Brittain's favorite indoor decoration.

opposite: The blue room is the "library" where guests can gather to sample some of Brittain's self-curated bourbon collection. The room gets low light so the Stones decided it was better to keep it dark for a cozy feeling of enclosure.

to an old house," says Rina, "and find a good deal of indulgent calm around so much greenery." The setting inspires Rina to cook for her guests from the bevy of farmers' markets in the area. While their home is still a work in progress, there is already so much to toast, first and foremost the union of a couple who knows how to spend their weekends. Says Brittain, "Mornings start late, and evenings end later."

# PERFECT PARSONAGE

New Preston, CONNECTICUT

PHOTOGRAPHS BY JOHN GRUEN

For an old Connecticut house, it was already pretty perfect. Built close to the road with fantastic views of neighboring cows out its front windows and the town's elegant stone church from the back, it had been kept over the years in lovely condition, and now a New York family with two young children who discovered it one weekend was ready to help love and usher it into the next generation. Built in 1780 and originally the parsonage to the church on what was previously the town green, very little had been altered over the years and much of its charming original features, like the floors, windows, and moldings, were intact. (If a window should crack, sheets of hand-blown glass stand ready as replacements.)

While they bought some of the antique furnishings from the previous owner to get a head start, the family soon infused their own

opposite: The dining room ceiling is so low that a chandelier doesn't fit, so oak-leaf tole sconces from Italy were installed.

opposite: Like many houses in the 1700s, this one was built very close to the road. It looks out onto a field where cows graze.

décor to bring some edge and personal style to the rooms. Now quiet punctuations of family history, like the 1820s goatskin surveyor's box belonging to a Texan grandfather who was a U.S. congressman, or the grandmother's beautiful worn rug, happily mingle with catalog-bought items that have been purposefully aged to a worn patina. Faux Roman frescoes scrubbed fresh out of the box with steel wool to dull their gloss, or a mirror whose gilded frame has been sanded and smeared with just a smudge of green paint from a favorite colonial collection always on hand in the basement, now boast graceful lin-

above: The original "keeping room" and still the center of the house. The room has its original floors, beams, molding, windows, and fireplace.

**165**

opposite: Plaques over doors came from a catalog and then the gloss was taken off using steel wool and dull paint. The chest was originally a somber mahogany until an artist was commissioned to distress it in a white finish.

eage. The kitchen, done entirely in old barn wood, offers its own airy repose, especially with its view to the extensive gardens outside. The cook of the house admits, "I think I take longer than I would ordinarily to prepare meals because I so enjoy being in there." Fried zucchini blossoms (grown in their own garden) with cheese, and peach crisp, made with fruit plucked from a poolside tree ("It yields odd-looking but amazingly delicious peaches!"), are house specialties. While food is being prepared upstairs, downstairs the perfect wine awaits, in a cozy, gracious wine cellar the couple converted themselves over time and aptly named "the grotto." The man of the house has spent many a holiday hour glue-gunning the doors with hundreds of wine corks, much to the amusement and amazement of his wife.

But cooking outside has become a greater lure since the family built a unique stone fireplace and patio area under a hundred-year-old maple tree. A local stonemason was called in to create a space that serves as the ideal summer gathering spot for cocktails, barbecues, and s'mores. And in the summer, no evening is complete without a stroll to the "firefly field." After dark, guests and hosts often walk down the road to watch the luminary show. "We know that someday the little ones will bring their own offspring here," say the owners. "This house has become more important to us than we ever could have imagined."

above: The family built the stone fireplace and barbeque grill to harmonize with the stone buildings on the property. In warm weather, they cook and eat almost all of their meals outdoors, often followed by s'mores.

# MODERN CABIN

New Preston, CONNECTICUT

PHOTOGRAPHS BY JOHN GRUEN

Originally designed in 1920 as a men's fishing and hunting haven, this log cabin in rural Connecticut was recently transformed into a year-round retreat for a Brooklyn-based family of six who own the surrounding farmland and find tranquility alongside the three-acre pond that lies in the heart of the property.

After winterizing it and adding bedrooms and bathrooms, they set out to create a feel that stylishly straddles both rustic and modern design. Midcentury pieces bought at 1stdibs.com and antiques fairs as well as modern pieces, like the catalog-bought Bertoia chairs tucked around a Renzo Piano walnut dining table, look completely at home within the Adirondack-style structure of stone and pine their architect, Reese Owens, helped them create. A second floor was created to house multiple built-in bunk beds in a streamlined space that

opposite: Nestled in a hidden valley, the house is the perfect combination of light and shade, breeze and protection.

opposite: The owners have always been drawn to fifties design and felt it gave the house a sophisticated and quieter style. The dining room table is designed by Renzo Piano with Bertoia chairs.

173

soothes with its soft hues of charcoal gray and exceptional pond views. "I wanted to keep it simple," says the mother and designer. "The building is interesting enough."

The main room, which comprises almost the entire first floor with its dining and living space, is ideal for games and puzzles in the winter due to its soaring fireplace. The active clan likes to spend most of its time outside, however, and the pond offers ample enjoyment: in the

opposite: Bunkroom cocoon cubbies designed to house four kids ages 6 to 18, come equipped with reading lights and outlets for laptops or iPods.

below: The elevated front porch is ideal for pond viewing and quiet summer reading.

winter they play hockey, and in the summer they swim and fish.

Warm days also bring the family's favorite activity: horseback riding. They take their John Deere Gator down to the barn and ride back to the house on the horses, often hitching at the cabin for lunch or cocktails.

Afterwards there is often pizza on the barbeque. "The trick is thin crust and get it off in a hurry when it's done," says the father. Soon there may be house wine to accompany their meals: the family has planted vineyards in the hills behind the cabin, which will become another reason guests and their hosts will never want to leave. The couple's retreat philosophy can be easily summed up: "Rise with the sun, play hard, and always wear boots: it really hurts when the horse steps on flip flops."

# STYLE FROM SCRATCH

Copake Lake, NEW YORK

PHOTOGRAPHS BY PAUL COSTELLO

W hen it came to creating a weekend re-treat for himself and his family, architect and interior designer Will Meyer stuck by his weekday mantra: "Design does not have to be expensive or complicated to have integrity." In fact, the uber-sleek single-story home he ultimately built on a hilltop overlooking Lake Copake in New York State is profuse with veracious style, lacking anything remotely frou-frou. Which does not mean that this abode lacks charm, wit, or warmth. One need only sit down on the Philippe Starck dining room chairs covered with sheepskin rugs from Ikea and feast on the homemade tortilla soup cooked by Will's wife, Kerstin, to understand that.

The house was built from scratch, with a mandate of capturing the lake and mountain views without overpowering the existing landscape.

The mostly glass, stone, and gray-stained wood siding structure succeeds in providing grand, seamless vistas of both the lake and the

opposite: Customizable storefront windows give the freedom to make Mondrian-like compositions with each glass wall for a variety of lake and mountain views.

Catskill mountains. "We used customizable storefront windows to give you the freedom to make Mondrian-like compositions for each glass wall so you can create a variety of views," says Will. Despite the grand sweep of Mother Nature outside, inside the house feels cozy and contained thanks to the omnipresence of tactile textures like wood, leathers, and faux fur, a décor Will describes as "eclectic modern that favors the everyday materials. There is nothing intimidating here." There is, however, much creativity and energy: the constant juxtaposition of the precious with the tangible, of displaying beloved art alongside Crate and Barrel. The couple furnished the entire house themselves, using much of their friends' work along with prototypes and used pieces already stocked in Will's warehouse. "We bought only when necessary and then usually for practicality."

Especially appreciative of the stylish set-up is the Meyers' three-year-old daughter, Lilly, who can often be found playing with friends

**181**

down the long hallways or trying to climb into the Nanna Jorgen Ditzel wicker chair that hangs suspended from the master bedroom ceiling, the ideal perch from which to watch the ever-changing light. House guests are also a part of the playful domestic scene. If they aren't helping Kerstin orchestrate her much-anticipated meals, they are enjoying the multitude of outside activities. And when it's time to come inside, there is the deliciousness of knowing there are bedrooms that seem to float in trees, and mahogany decks for those who can't bear to part from the fresh air just yet. And the only time the flow of joyful noise ceases is when it is replaced by the sudden and serene hush that happens when everybody gathered under one roof has at last found the perfect book and a nook in which to curl up with it.

# BEWITCHING BOATHOUSE

Berkshire Mountains, CONNECTICUT

PHOTOGRAPHS BY JOHN GRUEN

opposite:
The storybook 1880s stone boathouse, at the end of two connected lakes, enticed MacDonald for over a dozen years before she was lucky enough to purchase it.

"I knew some way, somehow, I was going to buy it, even if it meant jelly sandwiches for a year!" says Anne MacDonald of her Connecticut property set on five wooded acres on the edge of what is commonly called Twin Lakes. Perched on a rock ledge, the contemporary structure looks down through ferns, trees, and walls to a nineteenth-century native stone boathouse with a towering stone chimney and cedar-shingled roof reminiscent of Japanese architecture. MacDonald had to wait a long time until it went up for sale, and when she finally saw the sign there was no turning back.

It was the boathouse that bewitched this CMO (she's done stints at Pepsi and Citigroup) when she first saw it back in 1999 while kayaking. "To get to the second lake you have to go through two tunnels connected by a pond. It's very shallow, and most people don't venture

**above:** The wood paneling, window frames, and brick floor are all original to the building and MacDonald spent much effort to restore them to their original glory.

**opposite:** The lake beckons visitors and owner alike.

that far. But by kayak it's passable. I saw the boathouse on the shore in the distance. The closer I got the more enamored I became." And while the main house is where she weekends, the boathouse is her place for dreaming.

Once hers, she started by fashioning the 1970s main ranch into a glass tree house. It was four years before she embarked on the boathouse repairs: "I had to be sure of the spirit of the place first," says MacDonald. Luckily, the boathouse was in meticulous shape: the previous owners had replaced the roof and the interior, with original patterned brick floor, massive limestone fireplace, and hand-blown glass window panes with patterned woodwork, did not require any major touch-ups except for some cleaning, waxing, and polishing. "My goal was to get the building back to its original soul, but to add some modern aspects and make it self-contained," says MacDonald. As local fisherman silently observed from the water, MacDonald knew that the building had special significance, not just to her but to the entire community. Taking great care to locate local stone from the same quarry in a soon-to-be dismantled lighthouse, she added a bathroom and kitchen.

When it came to décor, MacDonald believes that "spaces should serve as a set for the play you would like to unfold. Then you increase the chances that it will."

The interior design firm Cassidy & Teti created a clean and serene aesthetic with an eye toward a European sensibility. Even though the boathouse was on the water, MacDonald wanted furnishings that were substantial, combining fabrics and textures in a luxurious way. Key was lighting to add drama to the richness of the wood and to highlight the vaulted ceiling and the stone. A high-sided George Smith couch upholstered in carpet and difficult to integrate into most rooms, found the ideal spot in front of the fireplace. MacDonald fabricated a large table from old French floorboards to accommodate ten chairs and long dinner conversations. A fish-eye mirror on the stone wall reflects nature's continual display. "Everyone had to have a water view," says MacDonald.

Outside, paths wind down to the lake from the house and afford gradual discovery of the boathouse one elevation at a time. But it is the lake just beyond that is the real star of the show. "It is the most alive piece of the setting," says MacDonald. "It is mood changing. I would find it hard not to live on water from now on." A typical summer day

opposite: The dining area used to be the water entry for boats but now is its own dedicated space for entertaining on the edge of the lake.

opposite: The living area centers around the large limestone fireplace. A George Smith sofa covered in kilim carpet is the perfect piece for the large space. The mix of stone, wood and rich fabrics achieves the old but contemporary feel MacDonald desired.

this page: Working with a local mason to help her renovate her boathouse, MacDonald found stone of the same quality and type in a lighthouse that was being dismantled. The floating wall holds a large frog-eye mirror that adds drama and a reflection of the lake beyond.

includes kayaking over to the marina for pancakes, then swimming the afternoon away, followed by a quick wash-up in the boathouse's stone shower before dinner. In the winter the boathouse fireplace keeps everyone warm after ice skating, cross-country skiing, or a game of ice hockey. No matter the season, dinners have a communal feeling, featuring seasonal ingredients, with young and old cooking together. "All pitch in to clean the dishes as the discussion continues late into the night," says MacDonald. "This place is set up with so many spaces that you can be social or alone to enjoy a book or nap. That was one of my desires for the property, to be able to go back and forth from solitude to social with no effort." There is joy in connecting to a place that feels worlds apart from civilization and yet right in tune. Says MacDonald: "That is what I believe every person's designated place needs to do: comfort, calm, inspire, rejuvenate, and restore."

# LAKE LOVE AFFAIR

New Preston, CONNECTICUT

PHOTOGRAPHS BY JOHN GRUEN

Why on earth would a family of two hard-working adults and their two harder-playing boys purchase and entirely renovate a weekend cottage located just fifteen minutes from their full-time home? We had already spent ten years nurturing an 1800s Colonial nestled under two-hundred-year-old oak trees from frumpy spinster into elegant matriarch that gave us year-round pleasure. So how could a bedraggled 1970s shingled cottage inspire us to walk the renovation gangplank once again? Three words: location, location, location.

Just set back from Lake Waramaug and cocooned by rolling hills where the serene yellow light undulates as if in Lake Cuomo, not north-western Connecticut, the cottage seemed to be in a patient slumber, waiting to arise from its spell of neglect. My husband, Eric, an emergency room doctor who finds pleasure in picking out bathroom fixtures and

opposite: Susanna Salk based the living room color palette on brown, orange, and beige, which she felt was modern and comforting. Orange leather chairs were found on eBay and the rest of the furniture all from online catalogs.

194

opposite: Visual
details of family life
are arranged on an
oversized metallic
chalkboard in the
kitchen.

this page: Sandstone
was selected for all
the kitchen counters
and paired with lots
of white to give the
new layout a clean and
modern edge.

opposite: A child's room is filled with exotic patterns to keep the feeling lively and playfully grown up.

this page: The old "Private Road" sign is kept more for its patina than message.

reconfiguring roof lines, was nonplussed and practically tore through the brambles to plant a kiss on his patient princess. I, too, was charmed. With her circuitous layout, it didn't take much to imagine where to add French doors, windows, and skylights to let all that glorious lake light in. A real upstairs master bedroom with peek-a-boo views of the water could be laid atop the current sun porch, which also needed a complete update to become a year-round eating area. A lap pool placed just outside the living room's new doors would become the house's ultimate accessory. The walls would be painted bright white and the wood floors stained dark chocolate. But what about the style of the rooms? The lake house was small, so it had to have a cohesive feel to maximize the visual

opposite: Susanna likes to keep her jewelry—most made by her sister-in-law Pia—displayed in decorative bowls and trays.

this page: The lake is a constant yet ever-changing source of inspiration and recreation.

opposite: Modern art bought on the Internet gives a white wall the perfect punch of color.

flow. I had never considered modern furniture before (our other home being filled mostly with antiques), but now I realized that its clean, graphic shapes could be ideal, even liberating. I didn't have time to visit stores, nor did I have the budget for a decorator. So through catalogs and Web sites, I decorated all ten rooms of the new house from inside the existing one, feeling a little as if I was cheating on my first beloved.

We moved in on Memorial Day weekend, and the boys and I fell asleep to the sound of Eric's drill busily building our life from the tiny pages of cryptic furniture directions. Nothing daunted him: when estimates for the lake dock proved exorbitant, Eric built one by hand with feverish abandon to house the used motorboat he had bought when

snow was still on the ground. I strung a hammock between two apple trees to encourage him to take breaks, but secretly I was thrilled with our pace: he'd finished painting the bookshelves just as my order of Penguin classics from Amazon arrived to fill them.

And then, it stopped. Our project suddenly became a home. We had our first dinner party. We christened the boat, and a dear friend brought us water skis. We biked laps around the lake and hiked to the hilltops from our backyard. The yin-and-yang contentment of feeling so rooted in our new home and yet on vacation made us all feel giddy. Or were we only giddy because we knew that our wedding china, and our childhood stuffed animals, were safely awaiting our return? Fall just dropped its first leaf into the pool, and we will move back soon. I am already feeling nostalgic for a place that hadn't even existed in my life a year earlier and nervous about reentering the one where I spent a decade of wonderful times. How can where we hang our coats be so comforting and complex? As I watch my boys pack up the car, ready for anything the next day brings, I realize it's not just about the house. It's about this time in our lives. Our children are young, and and we still have the luxury of all waking up and falling asleep under one roof. Whether it's painted white or pomegranate red, in the end, is secondary.

North East, PENNSYLVANIA

PHOTOGRAPHS BY MATTHEW HRANEK

I n northeast Pennsylvania a forest retreat within a week-end retreat awaits acclaimed designer Todd Oldham. He built the tree house as a way to escape a busy schedule that takes him around the globe and to fulfill a childhood dream of living closer to the sky—in this case, sixty feet closer. He had been vacationing in his weekend home for a year before he chose the wooded spot (with the help of an arborist, who advised him on the sight lines) about five acres away from the main house. The cottage is nestled in a grove of white pine trees and accessed via a four-foot-wide walkway winding 360 degrees around the structure. It took a builder four months to construct this elegant aerie out of steel, glass, aluminum, and wood, which was then coated with a transparent stain on top of the layered siding of white pine with its bark intact. The roof was then trimmed in a cheerful green.

Oldham designed the interiors himself to achieve a look distinct from that of his main house, a modern design mainly comprised of center block, aluminum, and concrete. Here, naturally lightweight materials abound to create a cozy nook with a distinctly poised style, which Oldham aptly calls "plush tree house." The fifteen-foot square interior boasts a ceiling height of the same proportion. A sleeping

opposite: Designer Todd Oldham's tree house fulfills his dream of living closer to the sky. He chose the wooded spot five acres away from his main weekend house.

**opposite:** Oldham pieced together corduroy slipcovers for his furniture and randomly painted out certain pine paneling strips on the floor, using makeup colors as inspiration.

**this page:** No matter how small the space, there is always room to create a personal still life.

loft generously accommodates a queen-sized bed and is accessed by a
vertical wood ladder best scaled by youthful climbers.

While everything, from the thin wood paneling to the three-
eighths-inch cabinetry to the laminate tongue-and-groove flooring
is thin in matter, it still packs a substantial style punch due to the
whimsy that abounds. Pine branches cast in white metal decorate the
cabinets for coats and wood-burning kits. An oil painting of a man
now dubbed "Mr. Moonie" has been transformed into an art piece by
way of vintage pictures of animal species pushpinned across its sur-
face. Ever the resourceful designer, Oldham pieced together corduroy
slipcovers for his furniture and randomly painted certain pine paneling strips on the floor using makeup colors as his inspiration.

Now the tree house has become as central to Oldham's weekend

opposite: Inside form
meets function to
achieve a style Oldham
calls "plush tree house".

life as the main house. "It's the ideal guest room, hangout place, design studio, lunch destination, and so much more," says Oldham. "Anytime I have guests with kids, they all want to stay there." And his dog, Ann, loves to bark at any uninvited squirrel or deer that tries to join in on the fun.

After all the visitors have gone and the duties of hosting another fabulous weekend of "lots of nothing" leaves Oldham a little breathless, he simply heads toward the forest to inhale what exists in abundance all around: "The oxygen content in the treetops is so relaxing, no matter how high up in the air you are!"

**PHOTO CREDITS:**

William Abranowicz/Art + Commerce: 28–35, 65–69, 71–79, 117–123;
Paul Costello: 178–185, back cover; Miki Duisterhof: 135–139;
Dave Engelhardt: 154–161; Don Freeman: 103–107; Oberto Gili: 20–27;
John Gruen: 7, 80–87, 124–133, 162–169, 171–177, 186–193, 194–205;
Matthew Hranek: front cover, 10, 37–45, 47–55, 207–213;
Maura McEvoy: 9, 13–19 (permission granted, Meredith Corporation,
*Country Home* Magazine, July/August 2005);
Phil Mansfield: 146–153; James Merrell: 11, 109–115; Michael Mundy: 88–95;
Michael Partenio: 96–101; Geoff Spear: 140–145; Simon Upton: 8, 56–63.

**ACKNOWLEDGMENTS**

Profuse thanks first goes to my amazing photo editor,
Kathy McCarver Root for her immense talent and humor.
And to my Rizzoli editor Dung Ngo who was as supportive as he was insightful.
This book would not have been half its gorgeous self without the extreme
generosity of the home owners who were the
most gracious of hosts by throwing their doors open to me.
And to the featured photographers who so vibrantly captured the rooms within:
Kathy and I can't thank you enough.
Special mention also to the following people for helping
us gather the many images herewith together:
Stephen Boljonis, Karen Bussolini, Donna Cerutti, Marti Emmons,
Visko Hatfield, Gregg Lhotsky, Jessica Marx, Judith Miller, Jennifer Nielsen,
Frank Parvis, Barbara Von Schreiber and Landis Welbourn.
And to Richard Baker for making those images look so wonderful in the layout.
Much appreciation also goes to Linda Zelenko for
shining her style flashlight in the direction of many of these homes.
Finally, a call out to my three wonderful boys at home:
Eric, Oliver and Winston. Wherever we are, you are my retreat.

First published in the United States of America in 2009 by
RIZZOLI INTERNATIONAL PUBLICATIONS, INC.
300 Park Avenue South
New York, NY 10010
www.rizzoliusa.com

ISBN-13: 978-0-8478-3200-2
Library of Congress Control Number: 2008938980

Distributed to the U.S. trade by Random House, New York

PHOTO EDITOR: Kathy McCarver Root
DESIGN: Richard Baker

Printed and bound in China

2009 2010 2011 2012 2013/ 10 9 8 7 6 5 4 3 2 1